Angelika Schmelzer

Horse Talk

Contents

Imprint

Copyright of original edition
©2003 by Cadmos Verlag GmbH, Brunsbek.
Copyright of this edition ©2004 by Cadmos
Equestrian.
Translated by: Claire Williams
Project management by Editmaster Co. Ltd.
Design and setting: Ravenstein, Verden.
Photographs: Angelika Schmelzer
Printed by Grindeldruck, Hamburg

ISBN 3-86127-940-1

How horses communicate

When people communicate with each other it's usually fairly audible, if not loud. Stories are recounted, jokes told: there'll be laughter, complaints, discussions, sometimes arguments or shouting. At other times a secret is quietly passed on or a loving word whispered in someone's ear – in other words, there's a lot of talking going on.

The content of the spoken word can be supported and strengthened in a variety of ways, primarily using the speaker's body: a clenched fist, a shrug of the shoulders, a dismissive crossing of the arms add meaning to what has been said. The face also speaks volumes: the more intense and emotional the discussion, the more frequently are the eyebrows raised, brow furrowed, lips pursed or laughter lines creased. Speech, facial and body expression all work closely together, whereby the spoken word always carries the greatest meaning, with body language being used to support and emphasise.

For our horses though, it's quite a different matter. Conversation in equine circles is carried out much more quietly, takes place mainly without audible expression and is often therefore unnoticeable to us humans. With little effort but in a very different way our horses converse primarily by using their bodies to convey signals and meaning. A slight movement of the head can suffice to tell another herd member: "Listen, I'm the

Human and horse conversing – albeit in different ways.

boss here and want you to get out of my way now!", or to ask a companion "Could you please scratch me just there?" It's true that horses do use noises to communicate, however what we hear does not have the same significance and meaning as our own language. Equine conversations are carried out primarily silently, using different parts of the body singly or together to convey meaning. The way a horse's body is positioned or held, i.e. its posture, plays a particular role, giving

Ponies together: conversation without words.

Vocalisation – spoken language

Important information for the entire herd, for contact over long distances and to those out of sight is communicated through vocalisation: an excited snort signals danger and sends the entire group into a heightened readiness for flight. Stallions show that they will not tolerate any competition through their unmistakable whinny; mothers call to foals and greet them with a tender, soft whicker. Many horses also learn to greet their own human herd mates with a welcoming neigh. Often though this only means that a lonely, stabled horse sees the end of his 23-hour long stretch of solitary confinement with the arrival of his rider... Human contact, even with someone dedicated to their health and welfare, is no real substitute for contact with other horses.

Even if you and your horse can communicate with each other, you will never take the place of other horses as a social partner.

other horses information about age, sex, social rank and the mood of each member of the herd. These signals are continuously transmitted and are often virtually invisible to the human eye, besides being difficult to interpret. In other words, in the equine world, horses use body language in the same way that we use the spoken or written word, vocalising only to support physical gestures or where it is necessary to communicate over long distances.

Facial expression

Compared to the facial muscles of us humans, those of a horse are much less mobile, meaning their expressive ability is relatively limited. Despite this, experienced horsemen can read our four-legged friend's mood from one look at his face and can tell if he is feeling well, off-colour or even sick. The facial expressions below should not be viewed in isolation, instead they must always be considered in connection with the rest of the body and its overall expression.

Mood barometer: the ears

Horses' ears are tremendously mobile, enabling them to precisely identify the source of every noise over long distances. They also indicate to other horses (and people) what mood the ears' owner is in and whether and on what they are concentrating. Flattened ears should be taken as a warning or a sign of aggression, while relaxed, freely moving ears indicate an interested, relaxed and usually co-operative horse. When dozing, the ears will usually hang relaxed to the side. In general it is safe to say that ears point to where a horse's attention is focused.

Tension gauge: the muzzle

It is possible to tell from the muzzle whether a horse is relaxed, in a bad mood or even if he is in pain. When in a good mood, the mouth is soft, relaxed and mobile while with an ill-tempered horse it will be tense and firm. Pain, for example in the case of colic,

Ears are as much a mood barometer as a means of hearing.

The sensitive area around the mouth reveals much about current mood.

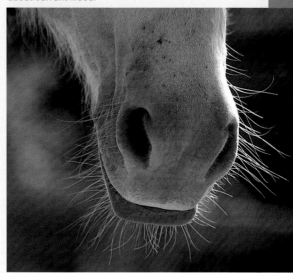

5

This Andalusian stallion looks at us without any signs of fear, albeit rather sceptically.

A window on the soul: the eyes

The eyes not only give us information about mood, but also tell the expert much about an animal's character. Large, open and calm eyes, with an interested look indicate that you're most likely dealing with an intelligent, trusting and self-confident horse. Bad experiences, fear and a lack of trust will be mirrored in the eyes. Wide-open eyes, showing a lot of white, are a sign of fear. Sometimes, though, this sort of eye occurs as a result of breed-determined pigmentation, for example in the case of many Appaloosas.

Body language

Horses use their entire body to convey signals to their companions. The body's posture and tension (or lack of it) show all herd members in what sort of mood a horse is, whether it is contented and relaxed, or unsettled and tense. This is seen most clearly by looking at a horse's silhouette, which itself may be used in confrontations with other horses, to intimidate or threaten. A shortened or contracted, higher silhouette indicates tension, while a longer, stretched out and lowered profile shows relaxation. When these outlines are created under a rider, we call them collection and extension. The rider's job is to create collection through elastic and supple tension, but without tenseness – a balancing act that isn't always successful.

can particularly be seen from the muzzle area: the nostrils will be pinched, the mouth will be tensed up and the teeth are likely to be clenched.

The legs too are used to communicate, especially in connection with fights or confrontations. The hind legs are used not only to kick, but to threaten action: if a horse approaches a higher-ranked herd member too closely, a hind leg will be raised to warn of a potential kick. In play and particularly when males are fighting, the forelegs play a significant role. They will be thrust out forwards singly or together while the horse raises himself onto his hind legs as matters heat up. This means of communication is the basis of high school lessons such as Spanish walk, pesade and levade.

A horse will move his head and neck in a swaying or snake-like motion in order to threaten others. At the same time teeth will be bared to underline the threat. A particularly expressive use of the neck and head can be observed when stallions herd their mares. A stallion will lower his head and weave back and forth with his neck to drive recalcitrant mares back into the herd.

Only by observing horses in their natural environment can their language be learned.

Elements of stallion fights were used to develop high school movements.

What is my horse saying?

If you are interested in your horse's language, not only do you need to be able to listen well, but you also need to be able to observe carefully. Only someone who observes horses as often as possible in their natural environment in the company of other horses, noting all their expressions and actions will be able to form a comprehensive picture of their language and then be able to use this knowledge on a daily basis for the benefit of both horse and rider.

Experienced horsemen and women know all about reading this complex and versatile language and are even capable of using it themselves. The methods used by many well-known trainers and performers – especially in the area of free or liberty dressage and loose schooling work – are based on the exact observation and imitation of the language of horses. Many of the horse's body language signals can be imitated by humans and used so that a horse can understand them without any difficulty whatsoever. Thus we have a means available that will allow us to communicate directly with our horses without the help of equipment or the language of the rider's aids. Knowledge of the

Foals and youngsters learn through play how to get on with each other.

horse's language helps us not only when raising and training horses, but also enables us to really get to know a horse and understand his personality.

A horse will only really trust us if he feels that he is understood. We can only interpret the language of the horse when it is put in the context of normal equine behaviour, for the way a horse communicates is a part of the total behavioural inventory of every horse. The development of appropriate social behaviour in particular, is unthinkable without mutual communication. Only horses that are kept in a natural environment (i.e. at grass with other horses) are in a position to master their own language –

both actively and passively – and only they will develop normal behaviour patterns. Horses that are permanently stabled, with no direct contact with others, won't be able to speak their own language properly and will misunderstand when other horses try to communicate with them. This particularly becomes a problem if horses have too little contact with others in their first three years, as it is during this time that the foundation for all types of equine-typical behaviour is laid, including communication. Anyone interested in learning the language of horses can only learn it by observing horses living in a herd in as near a natural state as possible.

First time under saddle: Praise gives a young horse a good feeling.

How a horse shows that he …

… is happy and contented

A happy and contented horse will have a relaxed body: when working there will be a certain supple tension in its movement, but it will never be tense. The horse can show his well-being by blowing gently through his nostrils, a relaxed chewing or by sighing and drawing deep breaths. Dozing in the company of others, the horse will drop his head and neck with half-closed eyes to underline his mood.

When worked, a happy and contented horse is more co-operative and learns faster than a bad tempered one. If a horse is at ease this has a positive effect on his motivation. A relaxed, good-tempered horse doesn't spook as easily, and if he does, will allow himself to be calmed faster, since a relaxed prevailing mood raises the threshold to fear-causing stimuli.

On the other hand, horses can suffer from bad moods and experience stress just like us. Stress can be caused particularly in situations where too much is being asked of a horse.

This over-taxing can relate to what is being asked for in performance terms, but can also relate to a horse's adaptability to various

Our horses are happy when their needs are fulfilled.

situations in his own life. Our horses are adaptable to a limited extent only, and if certain basic requirements are not provided, then mechanisms will be lacking which enable them to cope with these situations – leading to stress. All horses, as herd and flight animals, are dependent on the fulfilment of certain needs: the company of other horses, light, air, food and sufficient movement. If these needs are not fulfilled then their well-being will suffer enormously. This can be expressed in ill-health, but above all in the development of behavioural problems. Unhappy or stressed horses that are being pushed too hard can be recognised by the various forms of bad behaviour that they show – both under saddle and in the stable.

By using praise, a rider can trigger a feeling of happiness and contentment in her horse that serves as positive reinforcement during training, whether on the ground or when riding. A horse will remember the connection between a correctly performed movement or action and his positive feeling afterwards, created by the rider's praise. He will then try in the future to carry out the same lesson to the rider's satisfaction in order to earn praise again. A horse's clear answer to praise, i.e. his gentle blowing or chewing, shows a rider that her horse has understood her. If there is no such answer then the rider has probably not praised her horse in "horse language", in other words with signals that are understandable to her horse.

Foals explore their surroundings by mouth!

and then through examination by smell and touch with the sensitive muzzle. The hairs around the mouth are particularly important for this. They should not under any circumstances be shaved off; otherwise the horse will in effect become "blind" to close contact.

In the case of foals they will often check something out with a front foot, but they also like biting into anything that awakens their curiosity. Foals are especially curious as above all curiosity serves to make them aware of their environment and learn how to get on in it. Older horses too don't lose the ability to learn through investigation. Curiosity and the play instinct can be used and maintained in training through a variety of methods.

... is curious

Horses are animals of flight and therefore a hefty portion of caution always accompanies their curiosity. If something awakens a horse's attention, he will stand at a distance and try to form an exact picture of the source of the interest. In doing this, he will move his head up and down and from side to side. If fear or excitement is involved, this can be recognised through a tensed outline and sharply pricked ears. Sometimes too the horse will snort spasmodically. In contrast, the ears of a relaxed, curious horse will flick back and forth and he will approach the unknown object step by step with his neck well stretched out towards it. Adult horses check out strange objects primarily through observation from a distance

... is afraid

Fear is normally a temporary feeling, totally natural and even vital for survival. Dangerous situations, or situations that the horse perceives to be dangerous, create this feeling, which is then followed by some sort of reaction. The animal will run, shy, defend itself, or want to observe the event closer. Horse and human judge what is dangerous and what is not quite differently. Horses, as animals of flight, are always prepared to run away from frightening stimuli, while we humans will tend to analyse and then assess how dangerous the same situation is according to logic.

A horse that is afraid will sweat, his breathing will quicken and his pulse will race. If the cause of fear is a temporary stimulus – for example, an object by the side of the road – the horse will usually react by shying, jump-

Highly strung horses tend more towards fear than their calmer brethren.

Fear can be reduced through training.

ing to one side away from the danger, snorting and widening his eyes. If the dangerous situation lasts longer – a noisy tractor approaching – or if it appears to be a particularly great danger, then the horse will seek safety in flight, and bolt.

In cases of greater perceived danger, fear can become full-blown panic, with the horse's safety fuses blowing. He will run away in blind panic, will be totally unstoppable, ignoring all calls, attempts to calm him or rider aids, and won't stop for anything – even fences or roads. Less intense, but persistent fear is expressed by the horse passing small droppings frequently, which can turn into diar-

rhoea. The body is getting rid of any excess burden to prepare itself for possible flight.

Matters can become particularly dangerous in cases where the horse has nowhere to run. In a confined space, as for example in a box, tied up for grooming or even in the middle of a herd, the horse cannot flee into the distant yonder, but instead "blows up".

In dealing with horses we must have an understanding of their in-born reaction towards fear. There is no sense in punishing a horse in situations where he is reacting to apparently harmless stimuli with fear – we just have to grant that our four-legged friends react to and perceive things totally differently to us.

Flight is the normal reaction of a horse to situations it regards as dangerous.

The enquiring look on his face shows that this horse is not really scared.

... is going to take flight

Immediate flight from real or imagined dangers is the survival strategy of what was once an animal of the steppes. The horse's constant readiness to run away is its in-born instinct. The threshold to trigger this reaction is very low, with horses frightening easily at unknown sights, sudden movements or loud noises. Horses can take off in a gallop from a standstill, taking them a considerable distance from a danger zone very quickly.

Horses take flight in a gallop and their body and the way they hold themselves reveals much about their prevailing mood. If fear predominates, they will gallop in a flat outline with their neck stretched out and the face will show the typical mask of fear with wide open eyes, flattened ears and tense facial muscles. If curiosity predominates, then the muscles of the whole upper torso will be tensed, head and neck will be held high, the tail will stand up like a flag, sometimes even being carried over the back, and the horse will canter in short springy strides, or possibly in an elevated slow trot. The facial expression will also reveal curiosity: the typical enquiring look with pricked ears, widened nostrils is clearly different to the face of a fearful horse.

Once the horse's panic subsides, it will stop just as suddenly at a safe distance and look behind, possibly showing his heightened tension in further tense trot strides.

How long, how fast and how hysterically a horse flees depends not only on the horse's own temperament, but also on the reason for the whole panic. A rider can herself assist in keeping the horse's readiness to flee within reasonable limits. In dangerous situations horses rely on the judgement of their leader: if the leader runs away, then the rest of the herd will follow; if however the boss gives the all clear then calm returns. If trust exists between a horse and his two-legged herd leader, this will defuse many potentially dangerous situations.

Horses, including stallions, that are kept appro-priately will form close friendships.

Encountering new situations, sights or noises on a daily basis helps to reduce a horse's threshold level for a fearful reaction – in effect, desensitising the horse. It would be wrong to wrap a nervy horse in cotton wool since this will only make the problem worse in the longer term.

… feels part of the herd

Horses are gregarious animals and as such are very much like ourselves in a social sense. They form close friendships, lovingly look after their children, choose partners, quarrel with or are affectionate to each other. They will show the majority of their inborn behaviour only in the presence of others of their species, feeling really well only when they are with other horses. During their youth all horses have to learn to get on with their companions and continue to practise this throughout their life. Horses that are raised and kept alone do not have this opportunity and often find it difficult to reintegrate into a herd when they have been kept in isolation.

It is easy to recognise whether or not a horse feels comfortable in the company of other horses, as in the main all horses do things together. Whether grazing, dozing, running away or playing, mutual grooming or waving flies out of one another's face with tails, most horses behaving normally will do this in pairs or as part of a group. Disputes are usually limited to play fighting or hierarchy struggles

No normal horse will voluntarily leave
the herd to be alone.

Outside the breeding season, these two
stallions are firm friends.

Firm, long-term friendships between horses are not unusual and are indeed a part of
everyday life. They are usually only possible
however for horses in a herd, or at least where
horses are regularly turned out together, as
horses that are primarily stabled have neither
the opportunity nor the necessary social skills
to develop, build and nurture a close relationship with other horses.

Friendships amongst horses are usually
twosomes and are possible between animals
of both the same and different sex. Stallions
can build up close and non-aggressive rela-
tionships with other stallions when they are
suitably raised and kept. Male friendships are
usually forgotten though when mares enter
the picture: albeit often temporarily, close
friends become bitter competitors for the
favours of the fair maiden!

within a herd, and serious injuries are rare. If
anyone doesn't or can't fit into the group, however, and behaves inappropriately, then he will
usually be systematically shut out and/ or
withdraws himself.

... is resting

Just like other living creatures, horses need down-time to recharge their batteries. Thanks to an ingenious inbuilt mechanism, this need for rest is combined with the ability to be on constant stand-by, required of all animals of flight. For a horse, it would be inconceivable to retreat into a dark cave at night for hours on end as in doing this he would be giving up the control over his environment. Instead, Mother Nature came up with a trick thanks to which every horse can get well-earned rest without having to put himself in danger. Horses have a variety of different levels of rest at their disposal, varying in their intensity and thus their recuperative value.

The easiest solution to the question of how to take a break enables a horse to stand at rest. The horse will usually rest one hind leg – in doing so the hoof rests on its tip, resembling a shield. The muscles and bones of both hind legs are built so that the stifle can be positioned in such a way as to stiffen or lock the whole leg without any apparent exertion. Another way of describing this trick of nature is tireless standing, thanks to which while one leg takes the full weight of the hindquarters, the horse can rest his other leg, which is usually bent slightly.

... is dozing

In horses there are several gradations between being wide awake to being in a relaxed deep sleep: from standing at rest, through relaxed dozing to sleeping stretched out or half-reclined.

A horse's favourite time to doze is at sunrise – especially in the cold winter months, after eating or after hard work. A dozing horse will stand with sunken head and neck, eyes half closed, ears hanging relaxed to the side with the bottom lip slack and droopy. His breathing will be deep and regular. Often one hind leg will be resting, the croup tipped to one side. In the case of a gelding or stallion, the sheath will be relaxed as well. Horses like to stand together in groups, side by side or nose to tail, the latter being the perfect position to keep flies out of each other's face. Particularly in the colder months horses are often to be seen sun bathing. In the morning they will stand

This horse is standing at rest.

Horses prefer elevated positions for communal resting.

… is sleeping lightly

side on to the sun, to absorb as much warmth and health-giving UV rays as possible. This is noticeably different to their behaviour in bad weather, when they will turn their well-padded hind quarters into the wind and rain, to protect the more sensitive parts of their bodies from chills and saturation.

Even when a dozing horse seems to be completely out of it, his senses will always be receptive to alarm signals, ready to flee if need be..

When resting on his chest – i.e. lying down but sitting with all four legs pulled up underneath him, a horse can switch with ease between dozing and a light sleep. If he is dozing, his head will be held up and the eyes will be open. If he slips into a light sleep the head will droop down to rest on the ground. His eyes will shut and his breathing will become quiet and regular. At a warning signal from the herd watch or an unknown noise, the horse will be awake and back on his feet in an instant.

Resting in this position a horse can slip from dozing to a light sleep

A deep sleep is the most intense form of rest for a horse.

... is sleeping deeply

If conditions are suited, i.e. the herd is settled and one horse is positioned to watch over the others, a light, superficial sleep can become a more recuperative deep sleep. As the sleep deepens, a horse will stretch out on his side with his legs extended, head and neck resting on the ground. If you look and listen carefully, you may be able to see if the sleeper is dreaming. In phases the legs will jerk, eyes will move under the lids and quiet moans, snorts or even neighs may be heard. Horses get the most benefit from deep sleep. Often after only a short time – fifteen to twenty minutes – a horse will wake up, roll back onto his chest and stand up. Then he will stretch, shake himself and snort contentedly before resuming the duties of the day.

Horses can only rest when another herd members stands watch.

Frequently during both day and night every horse will take these short naps, which are especially important for health and well-being. It does seem that deep sleep is only possible when another member of the herd is in sight and standing watch. A horse will also sleep in his stable, both on his chest and stretched on his side; however, the deep sleep phases appear to be shorter and not as deep.

like us when we're in a bad mood, wanting to be left alone. Any attempts to get close or to get them to play will be grumpily refused.

Flattened ears and a raised hind leg tell the Icelandic pony that the Friesian wants to be left in peace.

... is in a bad mood

Even horses can get out of the wrong side of bed and be in a bad mood, sullen and lacking enthusiasm. When they do, they behave just

The mutual dislike between these two mares is unmistakable.

Whether being ridden or lunged, don't expect either co-operation or a willingness to work! Appetite doesn't usually suffer as a result of such a mood, however do expect a grumpy horse to guard his feed more vigorously and be more aggressive than usual.

Permanent ill-temper is always a sign that something isn't right in a horse's life. Often it may be a result of chronic pain – for example from an infected tooth, or a sign or wear and tear on the legs putting extra strain on the horse. The loss of a long-term friend or companion can cause grief, and with it a long-lasting mood change.

Asking too much – or too little – in daily work can also result in the horse appearing to be in a perpetually bad mood.

… wants to play

Horses like to play. As foals, they chase each other and play fight, but even adult horses show a well-developed sense of fun. Games exhibit patterns from a horse's normal repertoire of behaviour, albeit shown in a different context. Thus, for example, horses will chase each other or fight in fun. The very nature of play implies that there is no direct purpose to it, but in reality games are not without purpose. More than anything, they serve as practice for a number of varied and important abilities, and cement the bonds between herd mates.

Mares tend towards chasing and racing games, while stallions and geldings like to play

Play secures the bonds of friendship between horses.

rough, rearing, biting and circling one another before breaking off to gallop away. Masculine play fighting contains elements found in the high school movements: rearing, the slow elevated trot and striking out become the pesade or levade, passage and Spanish walk with appropriate training. As dangerous as these fights look, they really are harmless. All games are played according to strict rules and these ensure that no-one ever comes to serious harm. Contrary to common preconceptions, stallions, if kept frequently or permanently with other stallions or geldings, will play and form close ties of friendship with one another.

Problems arise when horses are raised entirely or mainly in isolation or are kept alone and therefore never develop normal behavioural

The playful overtures from the grey are not accepted by the Icelandic pony.

If horses behave normally, even apparently serious fights as shown in this stallion herd will rarely result in injury.

patterns for play. Such horses are often not capable of recognising playful approaches, instead interpreting them as an attack and reacting correspondingly aggressively. They can't express their own inferiority via the appropriate behaviour and thus withdraw from a confrontation, but equally cannot understand gestures of submission towards themselves either. The danger of injury in these cases is naturally much higher.

... can smell something interesting

There's something in the air: with outstretched head and curled upper-lip, an interesting or unpleasant smell can be tested and assessed. This easily recognised behaviour called the "Flehmen response" uses a special olfactory tool called "Jacobson's organ". Whether cigar smoke, urine or the smell of fresh droppings, it's not the nose but the much smaller concealed tool hidden under the upper lip that's used. Stallions more than most use this particular sense of smell. The scent of an in-season mare or the territorial markings left by potential challengers for his mares will cause

The hidden Jacobson's organ underneath the upper lip serves to identify certain smells.

... feels lonely

If a horse feels lonely, he will run back and forth and repeatedly and loudly call out to try and make contact with others. If this feeling of loneliness and desertion lasts a longer time, the horse will become increasingly unsettled and fearful, even possibly descending into a blind and unmanageable panic. As herd animals, horses are highly social animals, feeling safe and well only in the presence of others of the same species. The herd offers the comfort of protection, integration in a hierarchy giving each horse its place in the herd and allowing close friendships to be built and maintained over many years. Little wonder that horses that are kept by themselves often develop unusual and conspicuous behavioural patterns. Without constant interaction with other horses, without the protection of the

A mare calls loudly to her stable mates.

stallion to test the air with his head and neck stretched up, upper lip turned up with closed or half-closed eyes.

Unpleasant smells such as cigarette smoke, mouldy feed or car exhaust fumes also cause the same reaction. Some horses also show this response when suffering from colic, as an expression of pain. Even if it looks similar, the curled upper lip and laughter have nothing at all to do with each other!

This mare shows alarm, but also interest.

herd, a horse can become lonely and isolated and can't develop and express its inborn natural behaviour.

This results in a real pressure build-up since the horse's in-born social needs can't be fulfilled in the way Nature intended. A horse deals with this pressure by displacement behaviour: the birth of so-called "vices". Whether wind-sucking, weaving, circling, aggression towards people or being uncontrollable when ridden, much of this atypical behaviour has its roots in a horse being kept in such as way that its basic needs for companionship are not catered for. Stable vices clearly indicate that a horse may be lonely.

… is excited

In horses, just as in us, excitement comes in different flavours. It can on the one hand be connected with negative feelings, like fear or loneliness, and on the other hand with positive feelings, such as joy and happiness. If a horse is excited he will show it first and foremost through motion – typical of an animal of flight. He will run back and forth, shake his head, canter in short bouncy strides and take off bucking, stopping now and then to whinny or snort excitedly. Head and neck will be stretched upwards, the tail will be held up like a flag. The more excited

If a horse can convince himself of the safety of an object, then his belief in himself and trust in humans will grow.

… is working with you

Whether your horse is working with you attentively and willingly can usually be seen in the first instance by his behaviour, not in his ability (or lack thereof) to perform a set task. A co-operative horse will react willingly and promptly to all aids, providing he already knows and understands what is being asked of him. He will react with interest and curiosity to anything new. A concentrated and co-operative horse will focus all his senses on the object of his interest: ears, eyes, and his entire body will be ready to absorb and process information. However, a horse doesn't always focus his attention in the direction we want and he can just as well concentrate on things that are irrelevant in our eyes.

our equine friend is, the tenser his movements will be.

Excitement also typically affects the bowels, so an unsettled horse will produce droppings more frequently than usual, often in small amounts or even turning into diarrhoea.

If the excited animal has nowhere to let off steam, then whether it is being led, tied up or ridden, it will be unsettled, possibly taking the control away from his human herd leader. Concentration on work is always difficult for the excited horse, leaving the rider feeling like she's sitting on an unexploded bomb. Horses can become overwhelmed by their excitement, with their behaviour becoming virtually hysterical, especially when the dangerous stimulus can't be checked out – i.e. can't be identified as dangerous or safe.

This horse registers what's going on behind him with both ears and his left eye.

Eyes and ears are focused attentively on the people who have woken Harlem's interest.

The real barometer of a horse's co-operation are his ears. In the case of an attentive, concentrated horse, his ears will always be slightly in movement, playing back and forth, often with one ear focused on the rider or handler. His eyes will also look attentive, opened wide but not fixed wide open.

Incidentally, the attention span of a horse is similar to that of a young child. Young horses at the beginning of their training can give their work their attention for ten to fifteen minutes, while older horses can still only stay focused for about half an hour. As a rider, you should not only monitor your horse's ability to concentrate, but also your own. It will be difficult for your horse to concentrate on the task at hand if you aren't also on the job or are easily distracted. As a rider, you can only demand the same amount of readiness to co-operate as you yourself are prepared to offer. It does you both good to have regularly rest breaks.

This young mare is refusing to work with her handler.

working in a round pen, where a distracted horse will be constantly trying to look over the top of the pen, avoiding looking at his trainer. The sideways glance out of the corner of his eye tells his trainer exactly how unimportant she is! Any commands from this two-legged creature will be resolutely ignored; even clear reprimands bringing no lasting response. In this case the trainer has failed to create an appropriate working relationship and hasn't managed to enthuse the horse for his work.

Young, lively horses are easily distracted and it can be difficult to keep them focused. This can be dangerous, as they often appear

... has his mind on something else

In contrast to the previous point, if a horse is distracted or not concentrating, his ears will hang slackly to the side, his eyes will look uninterested, sometimes half-shut. His movements will appear stiff or uncoordinated and will lack any elasticity. The neck will be held horizontal and the head may swing. The inability to concentrate can be caused by illness, a lack of interest in the job at hand or by asking too much – although not asking enough can also be a cause. It is up to the human side of the partnership to realistically assess her horse's ability and set the work accordingly.

A horse will also find it hard to concentrate if his attention is focused outside his work environment, ignoring his rider or handler. This is shown most clearly when his attention is focused on something off in the distance. This is particularly noticeable when

Here the trainer intentionally works to focus the horse's attention on herself.

If concentration lapses, then it's time for a break.

The leader of a group of horses is no lonely tyrant using brute force to control his herd, but is instead a constantly watchful, experienced and considerate babysitter. Furthermore "he", at least in the case of wild horses, is usually a "she". The herd is led not by a stallion, but by the dominant or lead mare – in fact in the wild there is no such thing as a lead stallion.

Equally in a herd there is not just one boss but many. The hierarchy accords a place to each group member, with some members higher and others lower. Apart from the one at the tail end, every horse is the boss of at least one other. It is some consolation to the lowest ranked horse that he is not a sort of whipping boy on whom the rest of the herd can take out their temper, but instead is usually a particularly young, uncertain, inexperienced or weak horse that, although having lots of bosses, at the same time has many protectors, and need carry no responsibility. The horse on the bottom rung of the hierarchy ladder in an established herd will also often make friendships more easily, as he poses no threat to those ranked higher and will be seen as a safe play and scratching mate.

Higher-ranked horses have certain privileges over their lower-ranked colleagues. They have priority when feeding and watering, have preferential access to resting spots, take precedence when being turned out or brought in and when taking shelter. Where the leader goes, the others make way. If they don't do so immediately, they will be threatened with flattened ears, an unfriendly gesture of the head, a threatened attack –

to forget that you, the handler, are there at all. A sudden jump sideways can put the person leading him at risk, just as similar actions can when on the lunge or when ridden. It is good practice to ensure that the current of mutual concentration running between human and horse is never cut off.

… is the boss

Being the herd leader may have many advantages. Attached to the various privileges belonging to the highest ranked horse, however, are many duties and responsibilities.

Higher-ranked Candy threatens her lower ranked herd colleague as she is overtaken.

all meaning "Make way now!", a command that is promptly obeyed. If a rebellious subordinate wants to throw down a challenge, he will provoke his leader by ignoring this order. A fight will result, leading to a possible reversal of rankings. Mostly the hierarchy stays the same over long periods and only changes when higher-ranked members of the herd get older and weaker, while other horses gain in age and experience and thus go up the ranks.

Humans can fit into the equine hierarchy – or can at least try. The rider should be higher ranked than her horse in this hierarchy, being friend and boss at the same time. This ensures that horse and rider can form a partnership, while avoiding disputes of an equine nature and giving the two-legged partner the lead without great problems arising in every situation. The person must however always watch that she fulfils the responsibilities as well as the privileges of being the leader. Your horse must never be allowed to leave the stable, field or shelter ahead of you; a horse may not push or shove when being led and must absolutely never be allowed to rub his head against you. If you allow this and similar behaviour, then it will be clear to him that he is the boss, and huge problems will occur in everyday matters. Resorting then to the variety of training methods available – often in the confines of a round pen – to re-

The herd hierarchy also ensures that unavoidable quarrels can be ended through simple signals and without the use of force.

establish your dominance won't suffice – more decisive is the daily relationship and behavioural pattern established between human and horse.

... would like to be scratched

The best has been left to last: scratching. Horses simply love to be scratched and rubbed in the spots they can't reach themselves. In equine circles, mutual grooming is a sign of affection and an expression of close ties, but humans too can delight their four-legged friends with the same

pleasure. Horses regard intensive scratching, if possible in difficult-to-reach areas like the withers, under the mane, croup or to the side of the dock, as a sign of friendship. In

From the very start you are simultaneously friend, protector and leader to your horse.

What at first glance appears to be a threat is in fact ecstasy – recognisable from the extended upper lip. Why is he pulling such a face?

comparison, the often seen pat or slap on the neck is incomprehensible to him, although well meant by riders as both praise and as a sign of affection – albeit not in horse language!

Praise is much clearer if the rider scratches the horse's neck, crest or croup from the saddle, or from the ground, the chest, forehead or underside of the tail.

As horses are scratched, they will pull an easily recognised face – The upper lip becomes longer and longer, the eyes will half-close or turn up, sometimes the whole body will lean into the source of the scratching and it looks as if they might fall over. But beware – the ecstatic horse may want to return the favour, and that can end painfully...

Simple – Bianca is scratching him under his tail! That's so good!